WORLD'S FAVORITE

Easy Violin Pieces

CONTENTS

T0066656

AIR for G STRING

J. S. BACH

TRÄUMEREI

R. SCHUMANN

MINUET AND TRIO

W. A. MOZART.

OLD VIENNESE MELODY

TRADITIONAL

THE SWAN

Edited and Fingered by
M. GREENWALD

CAMILLE SAINT-SAËNS

MELODY IN F

ANTON RUBINSTEIN
Arr. by Calvin Grooms

Moderato semplice

14

FASCINATION

MARCHETTI
Arranged by R. Kail

Solo

rall.

THE ENTERTAINER

From *"The Sting"*

SCOTT JOPLIN
Arranged by R. Kail

VALSE TRISTE

JEAN SIBELIUS
Arranged by Calvin Grooms

Stretto

Lento assai

EVENING STAR
from "Tannhäuser"

RICHARD WAGNER
Arranged by Calvin Grooms

BARCAROLLE

J. OFFENBACH
Arranged by Calvin Grooms

SONGS MY MOTHER TAUGHT ME

ANTON DVOŘÁK
Arranged by Calvin Grooms

BARCAROLLE

PETER ILYITCH TSCHIAKOVSKY

arr. by M. Greenwald

HUMORESQUE

ANTON DVOŘÁK

Arranged by M. Greenwald

AVE MARIA

CHARLES GOUNOD

LA BRUNETTE

EDMUND SEVERN

ADORATION

FELIX BOROWSKI

POËME

ZDENKO FIBICH

SARABANDE

J.S. BACH

Loure

INTERMEZZO
from
Cavalleria Rusticana.

MASCAGNI

GAVOTTE from "Mignon"

THOMAS

SPRING SONG

FELIX MENDELSSOHN

GRAND MARCH
from "Aida"

GIUSEPPE VERDI

Fine.

Fine.

ANGEL'S SERENADE

BRAGA

VALSE from "Mignon"

A. THOMAS

KUIAWIAK

WIENIAWSKI

CRADLE SONG

M. HÄUSER

LEGEND

WIENIAWSKI

sempre cresc.

sempre cresc.

Fine.

LIEBESGRUSS

SIR EDWARD ELGAR

ANITRA'S DANCE

EDVARD GRIEG

LES RAMEAUX

GUSTAVE FAURÉ

SIMPLE AVEU

F. THOMÉ

SERENATA

MOSZCOWSKI

CAVATINA

RAFF

LARGO

HÄNDEL

SPANISH DANCE

MOSZCOWSKI

CARNIVAL OF VENICE

TRADITIONAL

Allegretto.